*Daniel Cohen* is the Founder and CEO of *Graduway*, the leading provider of alumni networking and mentoring platforms with clients across 40 countries.

A recognized leading thinker, writer and speaker in alumni relations, he has been named one of LinkedIn's Top Influencers in Education.

Daniel is the author of the acclaimed book 'The Alumni Revolution'.

Daniel chairs the Global Leaders Summit, a tri-annual gathering of leading global executives to discuss best practice and strategic trends in alumni relations.

# Table of Contents

# Introduction

Following positive feedback from my first book, The Alumni Revolution, I have been encouraged to continue sharing my thoughts on the biggest challenges and opportunities facing the alumni relations profession.

My work with Graduway, and hosting three Global Leaders Summits each year, exposed me to many thought leaders across the alumni relations world. I am grateful for their influence on this book.

In addition to 32 new and original essays, I have also included 13 of my most important articles that appeared in my previous book, The Alumni Revolution.

This book comprises a series of bite-size essays on key topics. You can read it from start to finish, or dip in and out depending on which area you are working on.

I decided to call this book, Alumni Therapy, because all work in alumni relations is ultimately about relationships. People see therapists when relationships are going sour or simply to strengthen important relationships. If we could view relationships with alumni like any other important relationship, then this would give us more insights on 1) diagnosing the root causes of relationship problems, and 2) identifying potential solutions to deepening and broadening those relationships.

With this in mind, I have split this book into four chapters. The first deals with the core issue and biggest challenge – maximizing alumni engagement. I then move on in the second chapter to sharing what I consider to be examples of best practice from across the industry. The third chapter takes a deeper dive into best practices – specifically focussing on career services and mentoring, which I believe could be a major part of the solution ib building deeper alumni relationships.  The final chapter concludes by looking internally at the alumni relations profession. It asks tough questions about the profession's relevance and where we need to be focused as a profession to truly add value.

Throughout this book, I make numerous recommendations of videos to watch, so the book is best read with access to the internet. (The easiest way to find the videos I refer to is by going to www.YouTube.com and searching for Graduway and the video title in the search bar, or going to the Graduway corporate website at www.graduway.com.)

Whether you are in the higher education space, K-12 or working in corporate alumni relations, this book is aimed at alumni relations leaders, irrespective of country, type or size of institution.

Like therapy, this book doesn't necessarily provide all the answers, but it does ask many questions which I hope will lead you in the right direction.

Alumni Therapy is an ongoing discussion and together I hope we will strengthen these critical alumni relationships.

*Daniel Cohen.*

# Chapter One – Alumni Engagement

# Alumni Engagement: Who Is Your True Alma Mater?

The words, 'Alma Mater', are commonly used to refer to the school that an individual attended.

*Yet have you ever wondered why the plural version, 'Almae Matres', is rarely used?*

Many of us have several education institutions that could be designated our alma mater including our high school, university or professional school.

Which begs the question, is there room for these institutions to co-exist and have separate but meaningful relationships with the same alum? Or is there a limit to how many institutions a single alum can support?

Is there a limit to how much time and money an alum can give to education institutions in general?

Moreover, if there is a limit, does that effectively mean that education institutions should be / are competing with others for the same finite volunteering and giving from the same individual alum?

And if it is a zero-sum game, where increasing giving from an alum for one institution may come at the expense of giving for another, how should your institution compete?

Finally, we have the difficult case when schools within the same 'mother' education institution could be competing for the attentions of the same alum and how best to manage that. Does alumni engagement come at the expense of another institution?

Lots of uncomfortable questions!

There is also a confidence problem out there with many schools doubting their suitability for attaining the top spot of the undisputed alma mater.

I often speak with K-12 schools (Kindergarten to 12th Grade) who lament their apparent lack of professional relevancy in the lives of their alumni. They ask - what role can a K-12 institution meaningfully play in the lives of their alumni?

On the other hand, I speak with business and other professional schools who lament their apparent lack of emotional connection with alumni. How deep can our relationships be when we have played a relatively small part in the emotional development of an alum and simply have been there at the very end of their education experience?

So, we end up with a strange matrix correlating professional relevancy versus emotional connection as follows:

| Education Institution: | Professional Relevancy | Emotional Connection |
|---|---|---|
| K12 | Low | High |
| University | Medium | Medium |
| Professional School | High | Low |

The solution may simply be about playing to your strengths.

K-12 institutions score strongly on the emotional connection and the pivotal role they often play in the development of alumni. They of course need to leverage this but begin to think harder about how they too can contribute toward professional relevancy in their alumni networks.

The Universities fall somewhere in the middle with reasonable emotional connection and professional relevancy.

The Professional Schools score highest on professional relevancy and probably least on emotional connection.

This is one of the posts where I don't have all the answers but believe there is great value in asking these questions.

Is your school the true alma mater for most of your alumni?

If yes, how did you achieve this?

If no, what were your biggest challenges?

I would welcome your thoughts.

# The 'What's In It For Me' Test

Are education institutions in denial about their alumni engagement?

Schools are implementing a variety of activities, yet are they making progress towards their stated goal of engaging alumni? Perhaps, they have lost sight of the basics of alumni engagement.

Engaging alumni should not be complicated. Fundamentally it is about providing alumni with a compelling reason to engage with your institution.

Let's switch roles for a moment, and put yourself into the shoes of your alumni, and ask the most critical question, **What's In It For Me (WIIFM)?**

What is my school **uniquely** providing **today** that is of significant **value** to my life?

**Uniquely?** Providing a value proposition that no one else can.

**Today?** The provision is real time, today, and not simply a nostalgic reliance on the past.

**Value?** Something that I tangibly see as a valuable benefit. Maybe quantifiable in monetary terms as something for which I would have even been prepared to pay to have access.

Understanding and articulating your value proposition to alumni lies at the heart of alumni engagement.

It can be daunting to answer the WIIFM question, but it is the first serious step to developing an effective engagement strategy.

The good news is that every education institution has the potential to provide a meaningful value proposition.

Your school can uniquely give access to an exclusive alumni network that will provide your alumni with both professional and social opportunities.

Professional opportunities can be about providing access to a career community: willing and able to help make introductions, mentor one another, and even provide job opportunities.

Social opportunities are about allowing alumni to join an exclusive social network that may well stretch across the world.

Each institution will express this value proposition in their own unique way.

Has your school articulated a value proposition for alumni engagement that you would be able to share?

What was the biggest challenge you faced in answering the WIIFM question?

# Picturing your Alumni Engagement

I received an inspiring email recently from Erica Yaeger.

Erica is the Assistant Dean of Development and Alumni Relations at the Naveen Jindal School of Management, The University of Texas at Dallas.

Erica sent me a copy of a picture of her institution's alumni engagement strategy and she kindly agreed to allow me to share it with you.

Take a look for yourself.

I love so many things about this picture. Where do I begin?

Firstly, the concept of having a picture to explain your strategy. Alumni relations leaders are often looking for ways to communicate their vision and strategy. What an awesome way to get buy-in from colleagues.

Secondly, I love the focus. It shows the school has serious intent about interacting with their alumni and clear priorities.

Finally, and on a personal level, I love seeing our clients using their alumni platform to support all those priorities, namely:

a) high quality and high impact programming,

b) consistent and meaningful communication and

c) alumni demographics and data collection.

Thank you, Erica, for sharing this best practice and allowing me to share it with a wider audience.

# Do Engaged Alumni Really Give More?

Ever wondered whether there is a correlation between the level of alumni engagement and donor participation rates?

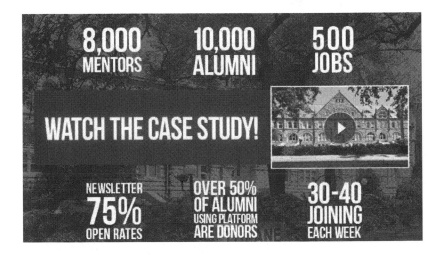

If you ask most education institutions, they will probably answer yes, there is a correlation: that volunteers make their best donors.

However, beyond that, it appears difficult to state the exact correlation and the direction of any causation.

Are engaged alumni more likely to become donors or are donors simply more likely to be engaged alumni?

A recent case study of Tulane University's on-line alumni directory and general alumni network provides us with more insights on this correlation. *(Disclaimer - their network is powered using alumni software from my company Graduway.)*

Please take one minute to watch this case study of the success that they have achieved engaging alumni (see Graduway's channel on YouTube: Tulane Connect Case Study).

Of all the wonderful statistics shown in the movie of alumni engagement success at Tulane University, there was one number that stood out for me.

Christine Hoffman, Senior Associate VP for Individual Giving at Tulane University said regarding the 10,000 alumni using their on-line network, "Over **50%** of our alums using the platform are donors. That is a significantly higher number than our overall donor participation rate."

**Over 50%** is an astonishing figure.

Especially when there are a very large number of alumni using the platform.

The Tulane University case study I believe is critical for alumni relations professionals everywhere.

Often, we are asked to make a 'return-on-investment' argument on why an education institution should invest in alumni relations. This used to be an incredibly difficult thing to do until now.

Tulane University's example is to show the massive value of every school investing in their alumni relationships irrespective of the direction of the causation between engagement and financial giving.

In a worst-case scenario, they have invested in building a career community that is disproportionately valuable to their donors. 5,000+ of their donors are using the platform.

In a best-case scenario, they are directly contributing through their alumni engagement to deepening and widening those relationships.

The old question of, *can we afford to invest in alumni engagement*, is being replaced with a new question, *can we afford not to?*

# Driving Alumni Engagement Via Digital 'Water-Cooler' Moments?

At the Global Leaders Summit at UCLA 2016, I had the privilege of hearing four world-class speakers present break-through ideas. Each idea was driven by technology and social media, and impacted alumni relations, career services, or the advancement world in general.

I recommend watching the four talks in full, but first up is Adam Miller in minutes 1-6. (See Graduway's YouTube channel: TED Style Talks).

Adam is the Director of Digital at Stanford Alumni Association and spoke about 'Harnessing Digital Water-Cooler Moments'.

A 'water-cooler' moment for a school would be when you become a topic of significant personal interest to many of your alumni. Adam quotes the example of the closure or renaming of an iconic building that sets off strong and vocal reactions digitally from alumni.

How should an education institution react when they are at the centre of significant alumni interest? Do you bury or leverage the story?

What struck me about Adam's talk is that he is right that these 'water-cooler' moments create massive alumni engagement and need to be leveraged and not feared.

The high alumni engagement levels show that you are making your institution relevant in the daily lives of your alumni irrespective of whether all the comments are positive or not.

As Adam put it, it is like the voice of the alumni coming back to your institution.

Moreover, we should be thinking of this in more strategic terms. How can we create a strategy of producing these moments on the one hand, and yet on the other hand, being sufficiently nimble to react as they arise?

Part of the answer is a required cultural shift.

We need to stop being afraid of our alumni and let them be vocally engaged.

Controversy can indeed be good. Alumni engagement is always good as it means they feel ownership for your institution.

The more we allow our alumni to be involved in the direction of our institutions, the closer our relationship will become.

What do you believe is stopping your institution embracing these 'water-cooler' moments?

Do you have examples of your own 'water-cooler' moments that you can share?  Why did they work?

I would welcome your thoughts.

# Engaging Alumni In The Wrong Order

Most professionals working with alumni for an educational institution understand that you probably need to have in place three things to effectively engage alumni on-line.

The issue is that most schools are engaging alumni in the wrong order by implementing three things.

What are those 'three' things and what is the 'wrong' order?

1. Data - schools usually build an internal database first to better manage alumni data. e.g. The Raiser's Edge, Advance, Salesforce etc.

2. Communicate - they then build marketing and fundraising tools to better communicate and transact with alumni. e.g. NetCommunity, iModules, Mail Chimp etc.

3. Engage - finally schools build an on-line engagement platform where alumni will network and interact with each other. e.g. Graduway.

Although all three components are necessary, they are being implemented by schools in the wrong order.

Let me explain.

Firstly, Graduway's own research has shown that on average schools are missing accurate contact information (email addresses, phone numbers) for around 70% of their alumni. You are not getting the full return from your new cutting-edge database if you are missing so much data. Your database is only as good as the data in it.

Secondly, the response rates to these smart marketing and fundraising tools is relatively low. Again, you are not getting the full return from these amazing tools if your alumni are disengaged and unresponsive.

It all starts and ends with alumni engagement.

If you are successful in engaging alumni by offering a valuable career network and community for your alumni, then they will reward you with two things.

Firstly, the higher engagement will lead you to have more accurate contact information in your database. The more engaged the alumni are, the more frequently their contact information will be refreshed, and the more accurate your database will become.

Secondly, higher engagement will lead you to have higher response rates from your marketing and fundraising tools. The more value alumni get from being part of your network, the more responsive and willing they will be to give back.

Better engagement will lead to better data on, and better responsiveness from, alumni.

And what to do if you cannot afford all three tools and platforms?

I would suggest that engagement should be the primary focus.

Let me conclude by showing visually how the three work together in the case of Graduway's preferred technology partnership with Blackbaud.

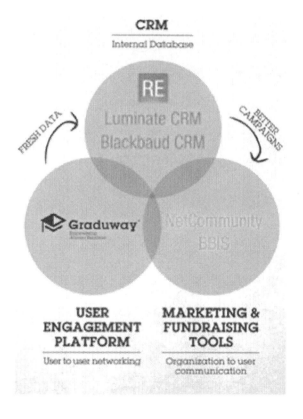

**Engage. Data. Communicate.**

Let's start engaging alumni in the right order and see the difference.

I would welcome your thoughts.

# 2 Golden Rules To 'Get Through' To Your Alumni

I sometimes feel we are over-complicating this whole alumni thing.

We are getting very sophisticated - accumulating lots of data, investing in hiring people, new IT systems, working extremely hard.  In short, we are throwing lots of resources at alumni.

But are we making progress in 'getting through' to our alumni?

I am not even talking here about why you want to get through to your alumni.

Institutions have different reasons as to why they want to get through to alumni - whether it's fundraising, gaining volunteers and ambassadors, building a career community or simply providing mentors to students.

The reason why you as an institution want to get through to your alumni does not actually change the methodology of how best to achieve alumni engagement.

So, let's get back to basics.

There are only two golden rules for getting through to alumni:

1. Physically Getting Through e.g. Do you have their correct phone number? For what percentage of your alumni do you have contactable information? Without fixing this basic first step, it is literally impossible to 'get through' to your alumni.

2. Emotionally Getting Through e.g. When you do get through to them on the phone physically, does the alum know why you are important to them? The reason cannot be just nostalgic that they studied at your institution 20 years ago. Rather the emotional connection comes from your institution playing a daily role in the lives of your alumni both socially and professionally. It's an emotional connection based upon the past, present and future. It's real alumni engagement.

There is a simple litmus test I would challenge any Alumni Relations professional to ask themselves when looking at their initiatives - will this help you get through to your alumni better, either physically or emotionally or ideally both?

If the answer is 'no' - maybe it's time to question whether there could be a better place to invest your resources to deliver alumni engagement.

I would welcome your thoughts.

# Can We Predict Alumni Engagement?

At the Global Leaders Summit at UCLA 2016, the second of our TED-Style Talks was delivered by Charlie Cumbaa, who is the EVP Corporate and Product Strategy at Blackbaud and spoke about 'Predictive Modelling and Alumni Engagement' in minutes 14-27. (See Graduway's YouTube channel: TED Style Talks).

For some time now we have seen the increasing sophistication in the methodology, analytics and use of big data generally to help professional fundraisers do a better job in targeting prospects.

In addition, we have seen case studies in the world of alumni relations of correlations between engagement and financial giving. (For those not reading these articles in order, see the case study I wrote about Tulane University on page 26 of this book – they have seen over **50%** of the 10,000 engaged alums using their career platform being donors.)

In Charlie's 'TED-Style' talk, he raises a new intriguing big data question for the advancement world: what if we could predict which alumni will be engaged?

For 84% of alumni relations professionals, as Charlie cites from a recent CASE survey, their number one goal is to drive alumni engagement. What would happen if we could apply technology and predictive modelling to improve alumni engagement?

What would happen if we could predict which of the alumni in your database had the highest propensity to both be engaged, and critically also the social influence to engage their wider network?

The consequences of smarter targeting of alumni could be to see a better utilization of limited resources and hence maximizing the level of alumni engagement.

Do you agree that it is possible to target alumni based upon their propensity to engage and ability to influence?

How does your education institution prioritize which alumni to focus on in terms of alumni engagement?

Do you agree that big data can play a significant role in your engagement strategies?

I would welcome your thoughts.

# How To Connect Emotionally With Alumni?

I hope the following simple pictorial story will resonate with you.

They graduate...

They become alumni...

They become part of a network...

Nostalgia.  Emotion.  Trust.

Engaging alumni requires these elements. These
are not 'nice-to-haves' but critical ingredients that will
make the difference in the level of alumni engagement
your institution can achieve.

When we look at our own giving, whether money or
time, the organizations for which we feel a greater
emotional connection will receive the lion-share of our
giving.

The more emotional we feel towards an institution, the
more engaged we will be: the stronger that emotion, the
wider and deeper the giving.

But typically, what happens after graduation?

The sad reality is that although many students will graduate with some emotional connection with their alma mater, this will fade over time.

So, what can be done?

Well, the trust and emotion your alumni feel about your institution is often represented by your brand.

If we were going to rank the world's leading brands, we would come up with the usual for-profit candidates - Apple, Google, Coca-Cola, etc. However, education brands would score highly if the rankings were done not on revenue, but on a more precious commodity, namely trust.

Each school has an incredible asset in its brand that needs to be properly leveraged.

The more you leverage your school brand, the greater the trust and emotion that will be generated and the greater the engagement.

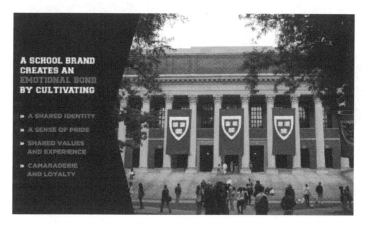

The surprise, therefore, is that some schools when engaging their alumni do not fully leverage their brand sufficiently. This is reflected in lower engagement levels.

Research by Graduway showed, for example, that branded school platforms are on average 40 times more engaged than non-branded ones.

The more branded you can make your on-line engagement, the more commited your users will be, and the greater the value of the alumni network becomes.

Is your current on-line platform branded?

How consistent and holistic is that branding?

And critically does the on-line experience feel to your alumni as if they have 'come home'?

Engaging alumni requires your offering to be more emotional, more branded. Only then will you start to maximize alumni engagement.

I would welcome your thoughts.

# Can Alumni Relations Be 'Digital First'?

At the Global Leaders Summit at UCLA 2016, the third of our TED-Style Talks was delivered by Andrew Gossen, who is the Executive Director, Digital, Cornell University Alumni Affairs & Development. He spoke about 'Digital First in Alumni Relations' in minutes 27-41. (See Graduway's YouTube channel: TED Style Talks).

**Digital First in Alumni Relations?**

Andrew advocates that digital has the potential to transform what we do - to take our alumni engagement efforts to reach not just the few, but the many.

This shift would result in alumni relations becoming more agile and opportunistic. And more de-centralized.

However, to get there requires a careful balancing act to combine the old with the new. It also poses a cultural challenge to education institutions in general, and alumni professionals in particular - can we make the significant shift in our thinking to embrace the concept of 'digital first'?

As Andrew points out, we don't want to lose what we have got, but at the same time we need to acknowledge that our current engagement efforts have a ceiling which digital can break-through.

How do we retain our existing programs which have served us well and fit digital into them?

If you were starting your alumni relations function today from scratch, how would the concept of 'digital first' change the way you structured your team?

What needs to happen to truly embrace digital in your programming?

In short, can alumni relations be digital first?

[NB you can read about the fourth of these TED-Style Talks in Chapter Three – Alumni Career Services and Mentoring.]

# It's Alumni Engagement, Stupid.

A Senior Alumni Relations Director spelled it out for me as follows:

Daniel, there are only two basic rules of fundraising... firstly, make sure for every potential donor you have a working phone number to call. Secondly, when potential donors do answer the phone, ensure that they are sufficiently engaged, before you even call, to know exactly why you are valuable to them. That's it. Simple.

It sounds simple but I sometimes see schools misunderstanding these two basic rules and building their alumni strategy in the wrong order as follows.

They answer the first rule of fundraising by saying: yes, we are missing basic contact information on our alumni, so let's build an expensive new database!

After a year and a lot of spent money, they have a beautiful new database but are unfortunately still missing basic and accurate contact information for much of their alumni body.

*In short, a great database does not mean great data!*

Schools then answer the second rule of fundraising by saying: yes, we have unresponsive alumni, so let's build expensive new communication tools such as websites, email marketing templates and donation processing systems.

*Yet great communication tools do not necessarily translate into significantly higher alumni responsiveness.*

To continue our original analogy - it would be like schools investing in an expensive new phone directory and buying the latest cutting edge Apple mobile and expecting this somehow to dramatically change their fundraising outcome.

It is not how nice the phone directory looks that matters, but rather the accuracy of the information within it.

It is also not the mobile phone itself that matters, but how the call is received.

Schools seem to be investing time and money in the things that by themselves will struggle to deliver the results required.

Instead, the primary challenge in my view, should be how to maximize alumni engagement.

If alumni are engaged, then you will be rewarded with up to date contact information (whether you have a great database or not).

If alumni are engaged, then they will respond positively to your communication (whether you have the latest communications tools or not).

An effective alumni strategy lives and rests on alumni engagement. Without engagement, everything else feels much less relevant.

I understand that building a new database or website fits better within all our comfort zones and that alumni engagement is not easy to achieve. I also understand that by the time schools get around to seriously thinking about how to engage alumni, most will not have much money, time or energy left.

Yet we do not have a choice. We need the focus and priorities of alumni departments to be radically changed.

Let's put significantly more resources into alumni engagement.

To misquote President Clinton, "it's alumni engagement, stupid."

# Engaging Alumni: How Much Would You Pay To Be An Alum?

Try asking your alumni relations team the following question.

Hypothetically, how much would an average alum be willing to pay to be an alum of your school?

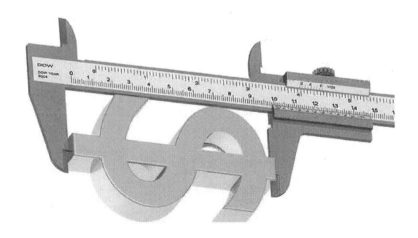

I know it is a question that most alumni relations professionals might be uncomfortable to answer as it over-simplifies what they do.

But its over-simplification is a key reason why I think it is a great question. It begins to help education institutions understand their unique alumni value proposition and how they are engaging alumni.

It begins to help prioritize activities and spending; to identify what you should continue to do, what you should start doing and even more critically, what you need to stop doing.

Let me throw some numbers around to demonstrate my point.

Email for life? Nice, but probably $1.

Quarterly magazine? Cute, but probably $2.

Access to an exclusive alumni network that can help me progress professionally. Now you are talking! This is engaging alumni and adding real value.

Sometimes the path to real change is not the answers, but simply asking the right question.

Are you brave enough to take the 'how much would your alumni pay' challenge?

I would welcome your thoughts on engaging alumni.

# Chapter Two – Best Practice in Alumni Relations

# What Are You Going To STOP Doing In Your Alumni Relations?

The classic 'Stop, Start or Continue' dilemma.

Most education institutions are great at the 'Continue'.

We all love the 'Start'.

But what about the 'Stop'? That one is usually a little bit tricky.

So here are my top 3 things I would 'Stop' doing in 2017.

1. Stop chasing mailing addresses for your alumni.

2. Stop producing physical alumni directories.

3. Stop providing 'email for life'.

Do you agree with me on these three or have I missed something?

And what would you recommend to other schools to stop doing in the year ahead?

I would welcome your thoughts.

# The Death of Email for Life

For me, 'email for life' is a symbol of how an education institution can become irrelevant to their alumni community.

For those of you who don't already know, 'email for life' is a service that many schools offer their alumni allowing them to continue to use their college email address after graduation.

Let's take a step back for a moment and try to understand what the real value of such a service could be.

For a few weeks or even months after graduation, I could understand why it may be useful for an alum who has not yet found employment to continue using their college email address.  But beyond this limited time, what is the value to alumni of 'email for life'?

Even if you were an alum from a very prestigious institution, when would you have the need to use that email address in practice?

I am suspect the percentage of alumni who actually regularly use such an address is small.

So, if this service is of very limited value to alumni, and probably hardly ever used, why do schools continue to provide it?

My focus here is not specifically about the pros and cons of 'email for life' but more about the underlying issue I think it represents, i.e. why would schools continue to invest their limited resources into less relevant alumni career services?  Moreover, what is stopping schools applying alumni relations best practices?

Firstly, I think part of the answer is that the old thinking prevails.  This puts schools at the centre of their alumni's world even if the alumni have moved on.

Secondly, there is a cultural reluctance to change. The easy option is to simply continue investing resources in the same things year after year.

Finally, I think there is a self-confidence issue. I suspect some alumni professionals do not believe they can offer something of value to their alumni so resort to the old ways of doing things.

I fundamentally disagree.

I believe there is a huge opportunity for schools to play a significant and valuable role in the lives of their alumni. This is two-fold:

1. Career communities - providing alumni with access to mentors, jobs and connections that can really help them individually and each other.

2. Life-long learning - providing alumni with access to both on-going professional development and

cutting-edge research made available specifically for them.

Schools have real potential to be relevant and offer value to their alumni if only they are willing to make that change.

It is time for the 'death' of 'email for life' and all it represents.

It is time for schools to start being relevant again.

I would welcome your thoughts.

# Alumni Website or Alumni App – Which Should Come First?

Every education institution is aware of the explosive growth in usage of mobile phones.

Successful on-line alumni engagement must give priority to the mobile experience.

To illustrate my point, Stratista cite that at the end of 2016, an average of 63 million unique visiting members via mobile. These accounted for 59 percent of all unique visiting members.

The conclusion would seem clear: Education institutions need to invest primarily in mobile - right? Maybe. Maybe not.

Despite the undeniable trend towards mobile, I believe there is a danger for alumni offices that focus too heavily on mobile.

I recently came across a school that was engaging alumni purely via a native mobile app.

The problem they encountered was that their alumni engagement efforts were shifting from trying to get their alumni to register and engage on the platform, to simply getting their alumni to download their native mobile app.

In fact, if you look at institutions offering only a native mobile app - you will see terrible download rates. It is common to see literally 10-50 downloads in total. (All the information is made available by both Google and Apple for their respective apps.)

I believe an alumni engagement strategy needs to be more nuanced.

The first stage is to encourage your alumni to opt-in. The focus here needs to be on ease of use. The alum needs to be able to register using your alumni website and your alumni app. And by your alumni app I mean a simple mobile responsive site that does not require any special downloading.

I have written previously on the importance of making the user experience of your alumni truly easy.

Your initial alumni engagement strategy must be device agnostic and easy for every alum to use.

The second stage is for those alumni who have already opted-in, to be encouraged over time to download your native alumni app. This is important as with 'push notifications' you can encourage alumni to increase their activity and engagement.

The two stages must be sequential if you are to avoid making a significant mistake.

So, to summarize. Alumni Website or Alumni App, which should come first?

Well I believe you need both and critically in the right order to truly maximize your alumni engagement.

Let's embrace mobile, but do so in addition to our web offering.

I would welcome your thoughts.

# Say Goodbye To Your Graduating Class. Forever.

The countdown has started.

It is already March, and for many schools, it is just 12 weeks until graduation.

Time to celebrate? Well not if you are involved in the advancement department of an education institution.

Let me be a little provocative. For what percentage of your alumni will graduation be the last time you ever hear from them again? 30%? 40%? Or worse?

For many of your graduating students the commencement ceremony will be the beginning of a lifetime of zero interaction with your institution.

The big question is why? Why do schools lose touch so quickly?

The technical answer is that the first summer post-graduation will, for many of your alumni, mark big changes in their personal and professional lives.

They will probably start a new role or job. They will probably move location. And of course, they will probably have new contact information. Within weeks all the contact information you hold on these individuals (address, email, phone number) will be out of date.

But that still leaves the underlying question - why? Why do schools lose contact so quickly even if these changes are happening?

The answer is because many schools often only decide to stay in touch with their alumni after they have already left.

In short, schools leave it too late.

In an ideal world, your institution will start to build its culture of philanthropy and alumni engagement not on the last day, but the first day of school.

For those interested in a strategic approach to this, please see Elise Betz, Executive Director of Alumni Relations from the University of Pennsylvania, who recently gave an inspiring keynote speech at the Graduway Global Leaders Summit. Her talk, **"Cultivating Roots: Building a Culture of Student Philanthropy and Engagement",** was a bold example of how a school (albeit a top one), can strategically invest in their culture of giving with an eye on the very long term.

However, what if your school is unable to think that long term and needs a solution in place within the next few weeks?

Here are three tips for you:

1. **Connect via social networks** - get connected with your graduating students via their social networks. Alumni may well change jobs and location but their Facebook and LinkedIn connection details will stay constant.

2. **Make them part of the alumni network now** - while it is understandable that you only want to reward students with membership of the alumni body once they graduate, it is simply too late. In particular, facilitating alumni networking and alumni

mentoring is critical.  Invite your students to join your alumni portal or alumni directory now. Alumni networks are for students as well!

3. **Give them a reason to stay connected** - show them before they graduate how being part of an exclusive alumni network can help them both professionally and socially.

The clock is ticking. You still have time to save your connection with your Graduating Class, but you need to get moving now.

Alumni networking seems to be a big part of the answer.

I would welcome your thoughts.

# Alumni Relations Budgets: We Can't Afford It. Really?

Running an Alumni Association or Alumni Relations Department is all about making tough choices - where do you invest your limited resources to have the biggest impact?

But to answer that question, you also need to be able to evaluate all resources at your disposal, including your people.

I recently asked two friends who are Alumni Relations Directors, one at a leading University and one at a leading K-12 School to share their annual budgets with me so I could better understand their budget situation.

What I discovered was two things.

Firstly – alumni software and technology made up at most 5 to 10% of the annual alumni relations budget they gave me.

Secondly, both institutions showed me their operational budgets **excluding** their people costs.  i.e. when they looked at their annual budgets and where to allocate their limited resources, they were not taking into consideration their human resources.

If you included the budgets spent on their alumni relations teams, technology expenditure was below 1% per year.

So, this begs the question, how do you balance your spend in technology versus people, in alumni relations?

The approach of almost discounting your annual investment in your team may in my opinion lead to counter-intuitive outcomes.

For example, I heard of a school this week needing to save budget, so it cut its externally provided software support costs, and got a more expensive member of their team to do this work instead.

Another example is building software yourself rather than buying from an alumni software expert.

Both these examples occur because schools are not making those tough choices by evaluating all their spend.

Prioritizing your resources requires a clear idea of your goals and the ability to measure and track your success. It also requires you knowing the impact of each line of your budget, including your people.

I am not advocating the mass reduction of alumni relations teams.

I am however advocating that we have an honest discussion about how best to spend our alumni relations budgets in its entirety.

Professionalizing our approach to alumni relations requires us to objectively re-assess where we invest our resources and yes, to potentially make some difficult choices.

# Is It Possible To Prove The Value of Alumni Relations?

Let me paint the scene for you.

You are an alumni relations professional sitting in a cross-departmental meeting. You are discussing budgets for the year ahead.

All your colleagues, one by one, are making Return on Investment (ROI) arguments to justify the budget for their respective department.

Your turn arrives. But you have a problem. How do you present an ROI argument?

How do you prove the value of alumni relations?

So, what are you going to do?

*The answer is not about Return on Investment (ROI), but rather Return on Engagement (ROE)*

The only way to truly make an argument for justifying alumni relations is to provide data to support your case. You must make a 'Return on Engagement' argument, and to do this you need to start measuring alumni engagement.

Chris Marshall, Senior Vice President at Grenzebach Glier & Associates, pointed out at one of our Global Leaders Summits, that there are three things every alumni professional needs to measure periodically:

1. How many alumni have attended at least one event?

2. How many alumni have volunteered?

3.  How many alumni have donated?

And then critically, how many alumni have done at least one of these three things stated above?

Obviously, bench-marking against peer institutions is great but if nothing else, you can at least benchmark yourself over time.

This is the first basic step in preparing an ROE case.

Once this is in place you can get more sophisticated by providing different weightings to different activities so you get a 'depth' as well as a 'frequency of engagement'. This can include regression analysis so that you can segment different levels of engagement and only then work out how best to leverage this ROE into more traditional ROI routes. Net Promoter Score and other similar techniques may also be a route that you can explore.

To see an in-depth discussion from the Global Leaders Summit on this, please see Graduway's YouTube channel: Global Leaders Summit 2015 Global Best Practice in Alumni Relations – Challenges and

Successes, and view the 31st minute of the Panel Discussion.

To conclude, it may be harsh, but if you have no data, it is very difficult to justify your value.

If you want to truly show your value, then start measuring your ROE and people will start to take notice.

Do you agree it is possible to prove your value?

What tips can you share on how you have successfully done this?

What do you think is critical to measure?

I would welcome your thoughts.

# 3 Steps To Ensure Your Alumni Relations And Fundraising Are Data Compliant

Guest blogger: Graduway's CFO and Data Protection Officer, David Whitefield.

Alumni relations and fundraising professionals are now routinely having to grapple with the challenge of complying with laws and regulations relating to data privacy.

The compliance burden is increasing and penalties for breaches can be significant. Storing and processing sensitive or personal identifiable information has never been more in focus.

What does this mean for alumni relations and fundraising professionals everywhere?

Similar professionals working in government or for large corporations may have the internal resources and tailored legal guidance to see through the maze. However, some of those professionals working in the not-for-profit sector may be struggling to know exactly how to respond.

So, let me outline three pieces of advice to ensure every institution remains compliant irrespective of the nuances of the new regulations you happen to be facing:

# 1. Don't panic

It is true that new laws and regulations are being implemented all the time regarding data privacy.

For example, in the Europe Union, the new General Data Protection Regulation (GDPR), introduces a raft of new rights and safeguards to EU data subjects on what can and cannot be done with their data.

This is a scary prospect especially given the lack of compliance may lead to financial penalties.

On the other hand, most new data privacy regulations are built on existing data protection laws. This means if you are compliant with the laws today, you should already be half way there.

In short, don't panic!

## 2. Ask the right questions

To map any gaps and understand what needs to be done to safeguard your data and your users' privacy, I recommend that you ask these fundamental questions.

1. What data is being collected and from which data subjects?

2. What is the data being collected and used for, who by and for how long?

3. Where in the world is the data collected, stored and used? Which law applies?

4. Within this chain of data custody, who is the party responsible primarily responsible for safeguarding the privacy of the data?

## 3. Choose compliant partners

Having the answers to the above questions will allow you to structure the correct and compliant solution.

But know that this is rarely done in isolation. Data privacy can have many related touch points such as Legal, Information Security, Marketing and Fundraising.

It is critical that you also understand to what extent both your internal and external partners and vendors are also compliant with new regulations. This also needs to be an important criterion when choosing future partners as well.

So, in summary, data privacy regulations can indeed be scary for alumni relations and fundraising professionals. But take a deep breath, ask the right questions and choose the right partners.

I would welcome your thoughts.

# Learning from Corporate Alumni Relations Programs

When it comes to Alumni Relations, it is always insightful to compare what you are doing with other schools' programs.

At the 2015 Global Leaders Summit (GLS) held at Oxford University, we had the privilege of taking bench-marking to a new level by learning and re-applying from the for-profit sector to the not-for profit sector.

The session at GLS was expertly chaired by James Stofan, Vice President at Tulane University. The two panellists were Sean Brown, Director, Global Alumni Relations at McKinsey & Co, and Leora Singer, Vice President of Alumni Relations at Goldman Sachs.

You can watch a recording of the full session on Graduway's YouTube channel: Global Leaders Summit 2015 Outside View: From the Boardroom to the Classroom.

I took two important insights from the session that I think can be applied to the education arena.

1. **What is your unique value offering to your alumni?** We heard the consistent message in the session of the need to provide a strong value proposition to alumni. McKinsey's focus for example is on supporting the alumni network, sharing knowledge and promoting alumni career services. I found it interesting to hear that McKinsey leverage their company expertise to the benefit of alumni by providing nearly 200 knowledge webcasts. What is stopping

schools providing better access for their alumni to the abundance of academic expertise?

2. **It is not about the money.** I found it somewhat surprising to hear both McKinsey and Goldman Sachs' alumni programs are in fact not focussed at all on how much new business is being brought to their respective firm from alumni. They do not even measure this. Their goal is simply about building a long-term alumni relationship - that is real alumni engagement. Every communication to every alum is focused purely on that goal. Should schools' alumni relations departments also be independent from the wider 'new business' goals of the school?

The session was a fascinating way to hear the raw principles of engaging alumni by viewing an institution that is truly different to yours.

# The Secret To Building An Alumni Social Network

Do you have a group of old, trusted, close friends that meets up every now and again?

Usually there is one person among that group of friends who organizes everything. They are the force that makes things happen. They are the ones who sets a date in the diary to go out. They book the restaurant. They ring around your group of friends to make sure everyone is aware of the final logistics.

Everyone wants to meet up but without this one key person it would never happen.

They are the people who make it happen.

They are your **playmakers.**

The playmaker role is also seen clearly in sport.

Wikipedia defines a playmaker as someone in association football or soccer *"who controls the flow of the team's offensive play, and is often involved in passing moves which lead to goals, through their vision, technique, ball control, creativity, and passing ability."*

Whether in sport or in your own group of friends, we see the enormous importance of the playmaker.

Alumni social networks behave in precisely the same way and its success will ultimately rest and fall on the existence of playmakers.

You can have the best alumni software in the world, the strongest brand, and professional and capable alumni relations staff, but without the 'playmaker' ingredient, your alumni network will not succeed.

At Graduway, we have analyzed the behavior of more than 300 alumni networks and have understood that the most critical ingredient to the success of the alumni social network, is the presence of 'playmakers' – or as we call them, 'alumni network ambassadors'.

These are the alumni who initiate discussions, who organize local events, post jobs and are most willing to mentor others.

They also normally represent 2-5% of the network size.

Without these alumni network ambassadors, your alumni social network will ultimately die. With them, they can thrive.

So how do you ensure that your alumni network has these playmakers? What do you need to do to nurture them and encourage alumni network ambassadors?

You need to do three steps.

The first step is identifying them.

You can identify alumni network ambassadors in a quantitative way by ranking your alumni according to who are the most active in your alumni network and whose activity exceeds a certain threshold.

You can also normally spot them by their behavior. These are the alumni who can sometimes be a little 'difficult' to deal with. They are the ones who challenge/complain about the status quo of the alumni network or who create their own 'rogue' or 'unofficial' network on Facebook.

What they are really saying with their behavior is that they want to be deeply involved.

The second step is to nurture and empower these playmakers. To give them roles where you can leverage their energy and activity for the good of the alumni network. For example, if your alumni network as groups, then these are the people who you appoint as your group owners or class ambassadors with extra administrative functionality in the network.

The final step is recognition. Your alumni social network's ultimate success rests and falls with these playmakers. Find a way to say recognize their valuable contribution.

You now know the secret to building a successful alumni social network.

What are you going to do differently to find, nurture and recognize these amazing alumni network ambassadors?

I would welcome your thoughts.

# Are You Crazy?  Don't Build It Yourself.  Buy.

So I asked the VP Alumni Relations, why did your institution build its new IT system rather than buy it from an external vendor?

And the answer went something like this...

You are right.  It was a mistake.  Our IT department is made up of very talented people.  And we decided to build it ourselves.  But it is not a scratch on what you are showing me.  In fact, I feel sick seeing what you are showing me, knowing that our product will never look as good and we have invested so much time and money.

I can provide some very practical arguments about why it almost never pays for an education institution to build rather than buy their own new alumni software, on-line alumni directory, website, database, networking platform or communication tool.

1.  Cost - it will cost more

2.  Time - it will take longer

3.  Quality - it will likely be less good, particularly from the user experience.

Even if one were to make allowances for the fact that your institution has truly unique requirements and customizations, I still do not believe that it would make sense to build your own alumni software.

I have also noticed a strange phenomenon. The larger and wealthier the institution is, the more likely they are to build their own alumni software and to be blunt, the more clunky and outdated their systems look. Wealth in this case seems like a distinct disadvantage.

I have sat with some of the world's best universities in rooms filled with their talented IT people who could build almost anything.

And here lies the root of the problem. Schools build because they can, not because they should.

The discussion over whether a school should build or buy is overtaken by the simple fact that they have enough internal talent to build. But this is not a sufficient reason to do so.

Let me use the crude example of a car. Would you build or buy your own car? For most of us this is a simple decision as we are unable to build, so the only option is to buy. However, imagine if you were a very talented engineer, would you really build your own car in your garage or buy one from an experienced automobile company?

Just because you can, is not a sufficient reason to build.

Rather the discussion should be centred around strategic focus. What does your organization do better than anyone else in the world? What is your unique expertise? Where should you be investing your personnel and conversely, where should you be utilizing external experts?

In our fast-moving world, I think the discussion is at long last moving decisively in favor of buying because of the emergence of one new factor, namely access to innovation.

I was speaking last month to a Vice President of Alumni Affairs at a very prestigious institution. They have very talented IT personnel and budget is simply not an issue. In the past, this organization had always built everything internally. Not anymore. This institution has decided to buy its new database from an established industry provider. Their motivation was simple - it is all about innovation. Using a database from Blackbaud or Salesforce meant having access to an ecosystem of partner vendors providing literally hundreds of innovative products each year.

This was the clear tipping point. Even the biggest university can no longer innovate in this specialized field at the rate of dedicated vendors. If cost, time or quality arguments do not work, then perhaps the final knock-out punch is about having continuous access to cutting edge innovation.

The days of schools building their own systems and alumni software seem to be over.

Has your organization recently entered a build versus buy discussion?

What was the deciding factor for you?

What would you recommend as the best way to facilitate such a sensitive internal discussion?

I would welcome your thoughts.

# Snapchat's $24 Million Lesson For Parent and Alumni Relations Best Practices

You may well have read about Snapchat's IPO last week that raised billions of dollars.

What you may have missed in the news is a fascinating story on how Saint Francis High School in Mountain View, California, made $24 million from the Snapchat IPO.

About 5 years ago, a parent of two students at the school, provided the school's growth fund with an opportunity to invest $15,000 in Snapchat. That $15,000 investment is now worth a staggering $24 million.

It is worth reading in full the beautiful letter that the school wrote to their supporters announcing the amazing news and their plans on how to sensibly use the proceeds to advance their strategic goals.

So, what can we learn from Saint Francis High School's heart-warming story for supporter relations in general, and alumni relations best practices? Let me suggest two:

## 1. Assess the true value of your community of supporters

All schools are trying to build a community of supporters. But how many can say they are maximizing the true value of their alumni, parents and indeed grandparents?

Has your institution properly assessed all the potential time, creativity, expertise and philanthropy that each of your alumni and supporters have to offer?

Understanding the true size of the prize of these critical relationships may be an important first step in resourcing appropriately this opportunity.

## 2. Invest in building your community of supporters

Building a community of supporters may well take time but it is a strategic necessity.

To unlock the true value of your alumni and parent relationships requires time and financial investment by your school.

I think there is also a subtle but crucial point with the example of Saint Francis High School about the order of alumni and supporter relations.

They invested first in their community, before they got anything back in return. And the return took many years and turned out to be massively disproportionate to the investment!

Engage first. Ask second.

What can make the community more valuable for your supporters? How should you best engage them?

To summarize, I hope the amazing story of Saint Francis becomes the inspiration for your institution to truly maximize the value of its alumni and supporters.

What did you learn from this amazing story?

I would welcome your thoughts.

# 3 Things You Can Do To Transform Your Culture of Alumni Giving

I think you are going to find this eye-opening.

It sometimes feels that schools may over-complicate their alumni relations and miss the basics on how to build a culture of alumni giving.

At the 2015 Global Leaders Summit held at the University of Oxford, I had the privilege of hearing Robert Caldwell, Vice President at Champlain College and previously Assistant Head at the Holderness School. Robert provided a masterful answer to the question of how best to build a culture of alumni giving.

Robert is an incredibly talented and yet humble person so will hate my placing him in the spotlight. However, I believe there is a significant greater good by sharing Robert's insights with education institutions across the world.

Robert mentioned three things he does which I believe could resonate with every school and make a big difference in building your culture of alumni giving.

1. **Tuition Bills** - tuition bills from Holderness School show first the full cost of the education, then deductions from various philanthropic sources including endowments and named scholarships, and only then the amount being asked for. This transparent approach makes it clear to the parent that financial giving is

something not to be embarrassed about, but a critical part of the business model to provide affordable education. It starts to lay the cultural foundations for future giving.

2. **Involving Students** - every donor from Holderness School gets a handwritten note from an existing student, irrespective of the size of the donation. The students state in the note unscripted what they love about Holderness and then include the sentence, 'I recognize because of you, this is possible for me.'

3. **Every Gift Matters But Need To Focus** - Holderness on the one hand recognizes and celebrates every gift made whether $1 or $1 million. On the other hand, it knows that 4% of its donors are probably responsible in absolute terms for 96% of its giving so ensures that campaigns for big amounts are targeted only at big donors. No one wants to be asked for something they are physically unable to give.

Please watch Robert in his own words, particularly at around 1 hour 2 minutes into the session (see Graduway's YouTube channel: Global Leaders Summit 2015 Global Best Practice in Alumni Relations – Challenges and Successes).

What do you think of these three insights?

What in your own experience is required to build a culture of alumni giving?

I would welcome your thoughts.

# Alumni Relations Best Practices: How To Ask Alumni For Money

Many schools outside of the United States, and in Europe, could be described as 'sceptical' when it comes to fundraising from their alumni.

On the one hand, they know the funding model of education is changing with the balance moving away from public funding towards alumni giving.

On the other hand, while many American schools feel comfortable fundraising for the worthy cause of education, most European schools appear awkward in soliciting funds from their alumni.

If I had asked a European school a year or two ago if they solicit alumni - the typical response would be a shrug that things are a little different on this side of the Atlantic!

Simply put, I think most European schools until recently felt they had neither the will nor the ability to create a culture of giving like that which exists in the United States.

Times are changing.

In January 2014, Melissa Korn wrote an intriguing piece in the Wall Street Journal on the changing culture in European business schools towards fundraising ('European Business Schools Get in the Fundraising

Game'). And I see that change in my day to day interactions with schools.

Schools in virtually every country in the world are realizing that they need to take a more serious interest in engaging alumni. Maybe not to solicit large funds today, but to begin to lay the foundations for tomorrow and critically to build the culture for future giving. So, what are alumni relations best practices in this crucial area?

Elise Betz, Executive Director of Alumni Relations from the University of Pennsylvania gave an inspiring keynote speech at the 2014 Graduway Global Leaders Summit at the University of Oxford. Her talk entitled *'Cultivating Roots: Building a Culture of Student Philanthropy and Engagement'* was a bold example of how a school (albeit a top one), can strategically invest in their culture of giving with an eye on the very long-term.

It may take some time, but I am convinced that someone will turn around 20 years from now and bless

Elise for the work she and the leadership at Penn did in investing in their philanthropic culture.

It is well worth watching Elise's keynote in full to see how she installed a tradition and culture of giving. (See Graduway's YouTube channel: Global Leaders Summit 2014 Elise M Betz). These are undoubtedly examples of alumni relations best practices.

I took away three critical ingredients that were needed to make this 'new' culture stick.

Firstly, to get students involved in this culture of philanthropy while still on campus - approaching them once they graduate is clearly too late!

Secondly, to have not just the support but the active participation of the leadership of the University in the campaign to build that culture.

Finally, the determination, innovation and perseverance to get the new traditions and customs to stick. As Elise memorably articulated, schools need to stick to the line that 'this is what we do here' when helping to bed down the new culture - 'a new tradition only takes two years to create!'

If you didn't watch it while reading the last chapter, I strongly recommend you see Elise's YouTube channel: University of Pennsylvania, Class of 2017.

I am a believer. I am convinced that if any school, and I mean any school, is determined enough, they could also build a culture of philanthropy and alumni engagement.

Do you have experience of building such a culture in your institution? What are alumni relations best practices in this area?

What remains the biggest obstacle in making a new culture of giving stick in your institution?

Do you agree that every school has the potential to create a philanthropic culture?

# Insights From McKinsey's Alumni Relations Best Practices

I had the privilege of interviewing Sean Brown at the 2014 Graduway Global Leaders Summit, held at the Said Business School, Oxford University. During our talk "From the Boardroom to the Classroom" Sean shared a unique perspective based on over 10 years' experience running leading corporate and academic alumni networks.

Sean is currently the Global Director of Alumni Relations at McKinsey & Company, Inc., where for the past seven years he has led the management consultancy's program to engage and strengthen its network of nearly 30,000 former consultants in over 100 countries around the world. Prior to McKinsey, Sean served as the Global Director of Alumni Relations at the Massachusetts Institute of Technology Sloan School of Management.

Please see my interview in full with Sean on Graduway's YouTube channel: Global Leaders Summit 2014 Sean Brown.

There were several amazing insights and alumni relations best practices that Sean shared in the interview, but I want to focus here on just three critical things that I took away as relevant for anyone looking to build and develop a professional network, be it a corporate or an academic institution.

1. **Offer a unique value proposition**- McKinsey do this by providing their alumni with access to

a) exclusive alumni networking via their official alumni directory where all alumni irrespective of their seniority are easily available to one another

b) alumni career services opportunities and top talent for recruitment which strengthens alumni engagement and builds the alumni networks and finally

c) ongoing access to the firm's latest thinking via twice monthly global knowledge sessions with cutting edge content for their alumni. I believe most academic institutions and corporations could provide a similar value proposition if they were focused on this as a goal and prepared to work collaboratively across departments.

2. **Provide a secure environment**- McKinsey have invested in offering a secure platform and the ongoing authentication of their alumni, which is critical in providing a trusted environment for networking.

3. **Create a culture of engagement** -Probably the most critical ingredient. McKinsey has created a 'pay it forward' culture which everyone is exposed to from day one. In fact, Sean's explanation of how McKinsey embeds this engagement culture from the moment consultants join the firm echoed what I shared previously from University of Pennsylvania's Elise Betz on how to build a culture of philanthropy and engagement.

It was truly inspiring to hear Sean describe McKinsey's 'joined-up' approach to their alumni relations. I believe that there is a significant opportunity for both academic institutions and corporations to also apply these alumni relations best practices, particularly in building that elusive engagement culture.

What do you think are the most important learnings from McKinsey's approach to alumni relations?

Do you agree that every institution has the potential to create a strong engagement culture?

Which is the biggest barrier in applying this approach to your organization?

# Chapter Three – Alumni Career Services and Mentoring

# The Case for Alumni Mentoring

The provision of mentors to students and alumni used to be a low priority for education institutions.

A service offered by the alumni career services department to the few.

Simply put, it was a 'nice to have'.

Not anymore.

Mentoring is fast being recognized as perhaps one of the most, if not the most, critical components of our formal education experience, and key in driving the long-term success for college alumni.

At CAAE Institute Winter Meeting in Scottsdale Arizona, I had the privilege of hearing a remarkable presentation by Brandon Busteed, the Executive Director Education and Workforce Development for Gallup, of a study commissioned with Purdue University. Brandon outlined what drives long-term alumni success and the role alumni organizations can have in impacting graduates' well-being.

You can download the full report 'Gallup-Purdue Index Inaugural National Report' at www.gallup.com and see an excellent article by Brandon on their findings ('The Blown Opportunity' on InsideHigherEd.com).

For anyone working in a University, I don't think it gets more fundamental than improving the long-term well-being (both socially and financially) of their graduates.

The Gallup-Purdue study found that **where** you went to college matters less to your work life and well-being after graduation than **how** you went to college.

The study found that students being 'emotionally supported' during college improved the chances of them being engaged in their work more than two-fold, and the chances of thriving in their well-being more than three-fold. Moreover, one of the most important ways to be emotionally supported is by having 'had a mentor who encouraged their goals and dreams.'

Just 22% of respondents could answer affirmatively that they had access to such a mentor. As Brandon put it,

> *Feeling supported and having deep learning experiences during college means everything when it comes to long-term outcomes after college. Unfortunately, not many graduates receive a key element of that support while in college: having a mentor. And this is perhaps the biggest blown opportunity in the history of higher ed.*

So why are schools not providing mentors?

Firstly, there has been a general lack of awareness of the importance of alumni mentoring and student mentoring.

Secondly, schools tend to think about facilitating mentoring in very resource heavy and non-scalable ways. The careers department will typically manually match and connect individuals to each other. This takes up a lot of time and is obviously not suitable if you need to do this for thousands of students.

The answer lies in a combination of leveraging your alumni and technology.

Your alumni are a readily available army of experienced and motivated mentors willing to help and guide your students. In fact, you probably only need around 5-10% of your alumni to volunteer to have more mentors than you need.

Technology has also changed meaning that you can literally provide alumni software or an alumni directory within days and enable students and alumni within the alumni portal to choose and connect with each other.

The onus will clearly remain on students to take advantage of the mentoring opportunities being made available to them. However, let's at least provide that opportunity to all our students.

Moreover, I believe there is an argument that facilitating mentoring should be a life-long service offered to students and senior alumni alike.

The case for mentoring seems clear. How will schools respond to this opportunity?

Do you agree with the case for schools to provide mentors?

Do you have experience of implementing such a provision and what were your biggest challenges? I would welcome your thoughts.

# Must Alumni Mentoring Relationships Be Like 'Marriages'?

A question for both alumni relations and alumni career services professionals — must alumni mentoring really be like marriage?  I don't believe so.

Let me explain.

For a while now I have seen two somewhat contradictory statistics.

On the one hand, in an average alumni directory or alumni portal, we have seen 70% of alumni say they are willing to be a mentor. This is an amazing and stable statistic as seen across hundreds of our clients' alumni networking and mentoring platforms.

On the other hand, we have seen the number of people who formally enter into an alumni mentoring relationship to be, relative to this 70% number, significantly lower.

So how can one explain this difference?

One possible answer is that although alumni are willing to mentor others, they themselves do not have a need for alumni mentoring? Possible, but this goes against lots of research that I have written about previously.

An alternative and more likely answer is that our definition of what a mentoring relationship means needs updating.

For some mentoring relationships, be it alumni-alumni mentoring or alumni-student mentoring, are an intense, formal relationship that is 'entered into' almost like marriage.

The reality is that most alumni mentoring relationships are not like that, and do not need to be structured like that. The 'marriage' model of mentoring, offered by alumni career services, may only be suitable for a minority of alumni and students looking for much more long-term advice and support.

I believe most mentoring relationships have a diverse range of intensity and formality.

Let me use the case study of Smith School of Business in Canada. Please watch first their two-minute movie on the amazing mentoring community they have created using a platform powered using the alumni software from my company Graduway (see Graduway's YouTube channel: Smith Connect Case Study).

What is striking about the success that the Smith School of Business has had building this mentoring network is the variety of alumni and student networking experiences they have facilitated.

Yes, they have enabled full 'marriage' type mentoring but they have also facilitated more informal mentoring such as being 'available for a coffee', 'willing to make advice' or offering to 'make introductions to my connections'.

In fact, if you look at the number of unique networking conversations then approximately 50% of the network has been involved in some form of alumni networking or mentoring.

When it comes to mentoring, we need to still believe in marriage, but perhaps we need to recognize other types of relationships.

Alumni networks need to be less well defined and more open to what alumni and students really want.

We may need to re-think how we offer our alumni career services going forward.

# The Dilemma of Alumni Career Services

There are several key stakeholders that have an important say in the relationship between an education institution and their alumni; Career Services, Development, Alumni Relations, Communication, Marketing and Admissions to name but a few.

However, there are two departments where at times I see some professional tension over alumni, namely Career Services and Alumni Relations.

I believe this tension is driven by two different viewpoints on student-alumni interactions.

Career Services is understandably focused on the student. In particular, how to help students enter the career of their choice while using alumni as an important resource along the way for mentoring, internships and employment.

Alumni Relations on the other hand is focused on the wider alumni body. Graduating students, although an important segment, will only make up around 5% of their total alumni. Their focus is much more on how best to engage all alumni and provide them with a valuable career and social community.

In short, for Careers Services alumni are a resource, a means to an end. For Alumni Relations, they are the end.

These two legitimate, yet different philosophies regarding alumni, can create professional tension if not managed properly.

Moreover, ultimately the danger of these tensions is the negative impact on alumni through miscommunication and duplication. Neither department wants to alienate what is both a valuable resource and an important end customer.

We have seen in recent years the emergence of a new department, Alumni Career Services as a natural response.

But for most institutions, they do not have the luxury of this new department, so how to get the balance right?

Here comes the controversial bit.

I believe some schools solve this tension through compromising between the two departments without ever properly defining who has the actual ownership on communications with alumni. The approach could be described as 'let's both own interactions with alumni and try hard to coordinate where possible.'

I think this approach is a mistake.

It results in duplicate systems, confusion, wasted money, and suboptimal student-alumni relations.

Even worse, what if alumni start to feel like a resource rather than a customer?

I believe schools need to clearly define who owns alumni. I also believe that it should be Alumni Relations.

At the end of the day, the alumni are the more important partner in the student-alum relationship. Students are the ones who need something from the relationship (contacts, introductions, advice, etc.). Alumni are there simply to give back and help.

As such the focus needs to be on:

- making the relationship as easy and straightforward for alumni as possible

- all communication to alumni should come via Alumni Relations

- the home for student-alum interactions should be the alumni portal (and not a student centric one!)

Alumni Relations need to own the alumni relationship in order that it always remains a healthy resource for everyone, including Alumni Career Services.

Who do you think should 'own' the alumni relationship?

I would welcome your thoughts.

# Bursting the Higher Education Bubble with Alumni Career Services

I attended the ASU GSV Summit 2016 in San Diego and heard an interesting keynote from Dan Rosensweig, CEO of Chegg.

Dan's presentation, which you can watch in full (see Global Silicon Valley's YouTube channel: ASU GSV Summit: Keynote with Dan Rosensweig, CEO of Chegg), discusses not if there is a bubble in Higher Education, but whether it is about to burst?

Dan eloquently explains all the data and analysis which I agree seems to point to a bubble and to the fact that we are probably close to the 'bursting point'.

The bubble appears to be due to an in-balance in the value equation for Higher Education. The high and increasing price for college is simply too high for the current value proposition being offered. Falling demand from students combined with over-supply from education institutions points to a bubble.

Where I have a different line of thinking, is not if there is a bubble in Higher Education, or whether it is about to burst, but maybe more importantly, what options exist for colleges to 'manage' this bubble?

There are three broad strategies that I think could be adopted:

1. **Do Nothing** - let market economics work their magic and deal with the over-supply by some/many institutions eventually closing their doors. If you believe that the 'bubble' is not evenly distributed and will affect other

institutions more than your own, then this could make sense. This might make sense particularly for Ivy League+ schools.

2. **Restructure** - another option is a combination of reducing prices for college education combined with cost cutting to make institutions more competitive. In short, increasing demand by providing a cheaper and possibly a lower quality product to students.

3. **Improve Value Proposition** - this final option involves looking at the underlying value equation being offered to prospective students and finding new ways to justify that premium price.

If I were a Dean or Chancellor, I would focus on the third option and I would invest in two areas that I think can improve the value equation relatively quickly and significantly.

Firstly, I would invest significantly more in **career services** including alumni student mentoring. A Gallup/Purdue University study last year pointed to the importance of receiving a mentor while a student in achieving improved life-time outcomes. Moreover, I believe the more a college can do to demonstrate how they provide superior career services, the stronger the premium they can justify. Parents will appreciate this as it is easier for them to quantify the return on investment from a college education.

Secondly, I believe investing more in **alumni relations** and in alumni career services. Your alumni are your institution's most important asset and building relationships with them is the equivalent of the business world investing more in their corporate marketing. Alumni are your brand ambassadors. The greater the alumni network, the greater the premium to your institution that can be justified. This also complements improved career services as your alumni will be an integral part of your students' career community.

Although I believe there is a bubble in higher education, I also believe this can be managed properly through increasing the value equation offered to students via career and alumni relations services.

Do you agree that there is a bubble in Higher Education?

And if yes, which strategy do you believe is the best way to manage this bubble?

Finally, do you agree that investing in career services and alumni relations is the best way to re-balance the value equation for students?

I would welcome your thoughts.

# How to get 42% Participation in an Alumni Mentoring Program?

Mentoring is clearly a buzz-word now in the world of alumni relations and career services.

Indeed, most education institutions would like to have a successful alumni mentoring or student mentoring program but may be confused as how best to make this happen.

With this in mind, at the 2016 Global Leaders Summit at UCLA, I had the privilege of hearing a joint presentation on how to build a successful mentoring program by Katie Davy, Executive Director, Alumni Career Programs and Partnerships at UCLA and Michael Schurder, Vice President Product at Graduway.

UCLA have used Graduway's on-line alumni directory / alumni software to power their alumni network.

Please watch the full session on Graduway's YouTube channel (UCLA Case Study: Building A Successful Mentoring Program Using Graduway).

The presentation is a great guide on how to practically build a successful mentoring program. Congratulations to the UCLA team for such an achievement.

I wanted to add three personal thoughts of my own on helping schools build a successful mentoring program, but with the emphasis on three 'mistakes' I believe schools need to **avoid**.

Firstly, I believe some schools become **metric obsessed** and lose sight of the goal. They would like to track and follow every possible click or interaction (many of which are not relevant) while forgetting to focus on the only metric that really counts - how many mentoring relationships are being formed.

Secondly, some schools tend to become **micro managers**. They want to co-ordinate and control every aspect of the mentor-mentee relationship. I believe the balance can get out of hand and stifle the natural interactions in a mentoring relationship. Your mentors are experienced professionals and do not want to be micro-managed. Schools need to facilitate these relationships and not micro-manage them.

Finally, I believe some schools focus their **efforts disproportionately on the mentee** (students) and neglect the mentor (alumni). In particular, schools make the classic mistake of building a stand-alone mentoring platform or alumni software, without any thought on what will motivate the mentor to actively and regularly visit that platform. A successful mentoring program needs to be built as part of a wider alumni/mentor network.

The result of these mistakes is that you can end up with a program that tracks every possible interaction, controls every aspect of the relationship and supports the mentee every step of the way and yet still fails.

Avoid these simple mistakes and I believe you will be much closer to achieving the type of strong results UCLA achieved.

Have you built a successful mentoring program? Can you provide feedback on mistakes you made and others can learn from?

Finally, which is the most important factor in your view for a mentoring program to succeed?

I would welcome your thoughts.

# Size Is Not Everything

I admit it. I am obsessed with LinkedIn and am a bit of an addict when it comes to collecting contacts.

I surpassed the milestone of 500+ contacts some time ago and am now rapidly approaching my 2,000th contact. But how valuable really is that collection of contacts?

In the social world, I have heard of people clearing out all their friends on Facebook and starting again. However, I have not heard of a similar experiment in the professional world. Maybe professional contacts are simply more valuable than friends!

Anyway, let's imagine a doomsday scenario. You log-in one morning to LinkedIn and find that your account has been magically reset and that your 500+ contacts have disappeared and you need to start again.

What next? How long would it take you to recover most of the value you once had from that list of contacts?

Or to put it more directly, how many of those 500+ contacts would you need to reconnect with to deliver most of the value that you once enjoyed from your professional network?

Probably a minority of those contacts will give you most that professional networking value.

There is a scientific debate about the relationship between the size of a network and its value probably most famously explained through Metcalfe's Law.

As your network size increases, the total value of the network probably does increase, but critically, by how much?

For most scientific laymen like myself, it seems obvious that contacts are not of equal value.

Although having more contacts will increase the breadth of your networking reach, it probably is not a substitute for also having a smaller number of deeper and more helpful contacts or groups.

The future of networking will be about how two types of networking interact and co-exist in your life.

On the one hand, we will continue to have these amazing networks like Facebook and LinkedIn that not only are our social and professional identities on-line, but also enable huge reach of connectivity putting in to practice the old dictum 'it is not about what you know, but who you know'.

On the other hand, there is a need in parallel for much smaller, exclusive networks that live to a different dictum, namely 'it is not just about who you know, but how willing they are to help.'

Alumni networks are a great example of how this new dictum of networking is going to make a big difference.

The size of your network clearly matters and will always matter. But, in addition, being part of a small, intimate group or one of your alumni networks, will provide extra significant value.

The age of alumni networking has arrived.

# So, should Alumni Mentoring Be A Dating App Or An Arranged Marriage?

I see a clear and positive trend of schools strengthening the career services they offer their alumni.

This is shown by a visible effort being made by schools to improve the collaboration between their alumni relations and career services departments. In fact, many schools now have a specific team devoted to alumni career services. This make sense as it is an area where schools can show a tangible value proposition to their alumni.

At the heart of this trend is mentoring - both alumni mentoring and student mentoring. In short, everyone is talking about mentoring.

Yet what is the best way to facilitate an alumni mentoring program?

Should a mentoring program be run on the traditional but resource-heavy approach of the school being the 'middle-man' and manually pairing off mentors and mentees? Or is this the place where technology should take the lead and automate the mentoring matching process?

At the 2015 Global Leaders Summit held at Oxford University, an esteemed panel were asked this very question. See the full discussion on this topic starting in the 31st minute (on Graduway's YouTube channel: Global Leaders Summit 2015: Future of Alumni Relations – Opportunities and Threats).

I think two key points emerged from the discussion. Firstly, which type of alumni mentoring relationships are most likely to succeed?

Eva Kubu, Director of Career Services at Princeton University highlighted the need to drastically change the way we match (whether manually or on-line.) The focus in her view needs to be about facilitating connections between alumni based upon shared interests, shared affiliations and shared intent on the purpose of connecting. In her words...

> *Most of the typical ways that matching occurs does not get to the core of what drives connections - namely shared interests and passions.*

The route to obtaining meaningful and authentic relationships is understanding the true passions of your alumni.

The second area of discussion dealt with how best to facilitate alumni mentoring, 'high touch' or 'high tech'?

Julia Sanchez, Head of Global Alumni Relations at IE Business School, cautioned a more balanced approach. On the one hand a 'high-tech' approach clearly has a contribution to make in the facilitation of alumni networks especially when your alumni diaspora is spread across the world. Julia highlighted the geo-location technology IE use in their app to help alumni find other alumni physically near to them. However, she also cautioned that technology alone would not solve all the mentoring needs, and cited specific examples of where her team had made important contributions to facilitating individual connections.

Where do you think the balance on facilitating mentoring should be, high touch or high tech? What is the right balance?

Is there a role for schools in the matching process of mentors? How critical is mentoring in building a career community?

If you haven't looked at it already, it's also worth seeing a great mentoring case study by Tulane University (see

Graduway's YouTube channel: Tulane Connect Case Study).

I would welcome your thoughts.

# Alumni Career Services: Your School's 'Social Media Day'?

At the Global Leaders Summit at UCLA 2016, I had the privilege of hearing four world-class speakers present break-through ideas. Each idea was driven by technology and social media, and impacted alumni relations, career services, or the advancement world in general.

You can watch the four talks in full on Graduway's YouTube channel: TED Style Talks, but this article focuses on Eva Kubu, who is Director of Princeton University Career Services and spoke about her recent 'Social Media Day' (see minutes 42-55).

'Social Media Day', I believe, is an inspiring idea that every education institution could implement irrespective of their size. It is particularly relevant for those involved with alumni career services or simply wanting to learn from alumni relations best practices.

In her talk, Eva outlines how Princeton University initiated a cross campus initiative called 'Social Media Day' to inspire students, alumni and faculty to better leverage social media both personally and professionally. In short, to take all their social media efforts to a new height.

The day included appointments with social media 'doctors', profile photo shoots and talks from inspiring alumni - all focused on how to leverage social media to learn, share and connect better.

Princeton were also able to specifically measure the outcomes of the day including metrics on the number of new tools or tactics learnt, improved career profiles, expanded knowledge of a new social platform, greater awareness of digital identity, increased confidence, greater understanding of using social media in different industries and making new connections.

Eva explained how 'Social Media Day' can be a major piece in the overall strategy of transforming alumni career services, from a 'menu of services' model to a 'career connection' model.

Princeton University, within 24 hours of this concerted social media effort, could literally reach millions of people.

Inspired? Hard not to be.

Well what is stopping you?

I believe the time has come for every school to consider running their own 'Social Media Day'.

# The Tech Revolution In Alumni Networks

I had the privilege of speaking on a panel discussion at the 2016 ASU-GSV Summit in San Diego, discussing the latest trends in student and alumni career services.

The panel was entitled, 'The Tech Revolution In College Career Networks' and featured alongside me were the following distinguished colleagues:

- Andy Chan, (moderator), Vice President for Innovation and Career Development, Wake Forest University

- Leah Lommel, Assistant Vice President and COO of EdPlus at Arizona State University

- Preston Silverman, Co-Founder and CEO, Raise

- Farouk Dey, Dean of Career Education and Associate Vice Provost, Stanford University

- Gordon Jones, Dean, College of Innovation and Design, Boise State University

Please watch the full discussion on Global Silicon's Valley's YouTube channel: ASU GSV Summit: The Tech Revolution In College Career Networks.

The discussion covered key questions such as

- Why we are today seeing such a focus on career services for both students and alumni?
- Are both technology and the rising cost of college, changing the employment landscape and the need for scalable career service solutions

- What are leading institutions doing to embrace this revolution ?

My own biggest learning from the discussion was to hear career services professionals in higher education talk about the shift of purpose in their own roles, as Stanford's Farouk Dey put it,

> *from being transaction providers of career placement, to providers of career education.*

Providers of career education should not focus on placing students into jobs but rather equipping and educating students on how to develop their professional community of mentors, door openers and support network which appears to be the main path to their career goals.

This got me thinking that probably the biggest obstacle to this technology revolution in college alumni networks has probably nothing to do with technology. Rather I see the biggest obstacle being a cultural one. Colleges need to understand that to successfully deliver on this new career services vision and leveraging technology, requires the end of the silo thinking around the management of students' careers. In particular, the silo that I see daily between career services and alumni relations that must be torn down.

Technology has a huge role to play in supporting the revolution.

Yet I have been left with the open question. Is the higher education world ready and capable of embracing the cultural changes, the cross departmental collaboration, required to unleash this revolution?

I would welcome your thoughts.

# 5 Big Mentoring Mistakes

A few weeks ago, I wrote a blog called The Case for Alumni Mentoring.

There, I highlighted the latest research by Gallup-Purdue University which showed that the key to students achieving long term success *after* college was having a mentor *during* college.

If, like me, you are convinced that all our students need a mentor, what is the best way to make this happen?

The answer lies in using a combination of both technology (alumni software or alumni networking platform) and a large group of capable and willing mentors (your army of alumni).

However, too often, I see well-intentioned schools making 5 *big* student and alumni mentoring mistakes. (Please forgive the Julia Roberts clip but I could not resist.) They are as follows:

1. **Not providing a scalable solution** - manually pairing off students with alumni, one at a time, is not a scalable solution and requires too many resources and man-hours. The goal here is providing *all* students with the opportunity to have a mentor. To do this you must provide alumni software where students and alumni can pair themselves off with each other, by the thousands, and without the direct intervention of the school. The school's role here is simply one of facilitation.

2. **Not providing sufficient value for mentors** - usually it is much harder to get mentors (alumni) rather than mentees (students) to join the platform. What is the value proposition to, and the motivation for, mentors joining your platform? As such, to have a successful alumni mentoring or student mentoring program, you cannot have it as a stand-alone module. It will only work if it is part of a wider alumni networking platform where there are reasons for your mentors to be engaged

and active such as jobs, events, photos, discussions etc. A strong alumni networking platform will lead to a strong mentoring platform within it.

3. **Micro-managing users** - there is a fine balance between facilitating mentoring relationships and micro-managing those relationships. Having connected with each other via your platform, your mentors and mentees are quite capable, to organize when, how and where they will communicate going forward. Features such as appointment scheduling, in my opinion, look both clumsy and interfering.

4. **Not making the mentoring specific enough** - providing willing alumni is a good start. However, the mentees need to know specifically what each mentor is willing and unwilling to do. Mentoring means something different to each of us. The more specific and granular you can make each mentor's willingness

to help, the more likely the mentoring introductions will be successful.

5. **Not making mentoring relevant for your community** - the type of mentoring offered needs to be specific and relevant to your community. For many, this is purely about professional mentoring by finding a mentor in your chosen industry or profession. However, for others, it can be social and even spiritual - students finding life coaches and role models that can provide valuable support through their shared gender, sexuality, ethnicity, nationality etc.

Mentoring is a critical offering for all education institutions.

I hope my highlighting these 5 *big* student alumni mentoring mistakes can improve our chances of doing it right whether you work with students, alumni or alumni career services.

I would welcome your thoughts.

# Chapter Four – Alumni Relations Professionals

# Making The Case For Funding Alumni Relations

The education world is under pressure.

Public funding is falling.  Tuition fees are rising.  Cost cutting is everywhere.

Yet I hear consistently from Alumni Relations professionals of how they are under-resourced in terms of both headcount and budget.  In fact, some would go as far as to claim that theirs is the most under-resourced department.

In such a tough macro environment, making the case for increasing funding is a challenge.

Speak to your Dean or Vice-Chancellor about increasing Alumni Relations funding, and you may get a standard response that surely there are other more pressing and urgent areas for investment?

We seem unable to articulate clearly enough that Alumni Relations is an urgent priority and not a 'nice to have'.

I think there are two main reasons why we are failing:

1. **Short-term thinking** - education institutions need results quickly from investments they make. Building your brand through your ambassadors is critical to the long-term health of the school.

2. **Measuring the wrong things** - the key performance indicators for leaders in education are usually student numbers, research or teachings scores and not direct alumni relations measures.

So, what can be done?

One route is to rehash our old arguments of how Alumni Relations will improve enrolment figures, allow the selling of more executive education services, and of course lead to greater donations.

However, I think it time for us to be a little more direct. The old arguments are falling on deaf ears.

Instead, one measure your Leadership will surely listen to concerns ranking.

The good news is that the major external rankings are increasingly putting greater emphasis on alumni feedback.

For example, Bloomberg Businessweek requires 30% of a graduating class to respond to its survey to qualify to enter their rankings. The Financial Times alumni responses contribute a staggering 59% of their ranking's weight.

So, in short, when you are making that proposal to increase... yes, talk about the long-term health of the school, and yes, talk about enrolment and development.

But let's be smarter. Let's talk about the short-term impact on rankings as well as the long-term brand building that will come from investing more.

I would welcome your thoughts.

# Don't Be Afraid Of Your Alumni

Let's face it, most Alumni Relations Directors are a little afraid of their alumni.

To some extent this is completely understandable. Unhappy alumni can be extremely vocal.

Some of you may remember an old blog of mine. It discussed the case of a certain alum from an Australian University who wrote a public letter on LinkedIn about how unhappy she was that her alma mater dare ask her for money when they had not been in touch for so long.

Yes, her negative blog received 10,000 views but schools must not draw the wrong conclusions from examples like this.

Let's start with two home-truths.

Firstly, it is a statistical certainty that when an education institution does any alumni engagement activity, there will be a small minority who give a negative reaction. Engaging alumni will mean that a small minority may even give quite a vocal negative response via emails and phone calls. Despite their noise, they remain small in number.

The second truth is that the clear majority of your alumni will probably *silently* be neutral at worst, and hopefully be very appreciative of your engagement activity.

Should the happy but quiet majority of your alumni be over-ruled by the loud minority?

I often find that some schools are so concerned about offending alumni and enduring their vocal response that it affects the frequency of their engagement. There is a fear about over-communicating with alumni that leads to a paralysis of engagement.

The logic almost dictates that it is better to engage less with alumni if it means reducing the risk of causing some negative reaction, however small, from a minority of alumni.

I think differently. Schools need to be more confident. Engaging alumni requires self-confidence in the value you are bringing to your alumni.

Schools need to put the vocal minority into perspective and concentrate their efforts on providing alumni engagement that adds real value to the lives of alumni.

The best answer to disgruntled alumni is to offer them engagement that is relevant and valuable to their lives.

Don't be afraid. Keep engaging alumni.

I would welcome your thoughts.

# Alumni Relations Best Practice: Are You Salt, Pepper or Cinnamon?

At the 2016 Global Leaders Summit held at UCLA, we were privileged to hear three of our most thoughtful leaders discussing the biggest trends and challenges facing the Alumni Relations profession.

The three leaders were:

- Howard Wolf, Vice President for Alumni Affairs at Stanford University (panel chair)

- Paula Bonner, President, Wisconsin Alumni Association

- Julie Sina, Associate Vice Chancellor Alumni Affairs at UCLA Foundation

Please watch the full recording of their conversation on Graduway's YouTube channel: The Alumni Relations Profession - Where Exactly Are We Headed?

There was much discussion about best practice in alumni relations and critical trends in the industry, whether it be leveraging technology, working better cross-functionally, or improving how we measure and communicate the value of our alumni relations efforts.

However, one moment in the conversation stood out for me when describing the biggest challenge facing alumni relations professionals.

Howard Wolf repeated the question that was asked of Stanford alumni in a recent survey, "If your alumni association was a spice in the kitchen, which would it be and why?"

The scary but probably typical answer for many of our alumni, is that their Association is probably a spice that they would never, ever, use.

If we tighten the question, and ignore the distinctions between Alumni Associations and the mother institution, the question really is how do we make ourselves essential to our alumni?

Are we a spice that is beyond its best before date and needs to be replaced?

Is it realistic to believe that we could ever be an essential component in the lives of our alumni?

Or do we believe we can be an essential conduit in the lives of our alumni. A spice that they will use often that brings real value.

The challenge is clear. Which spice will we be?

# Do Alumni Associations Really Want To Engage Alumni?

Ask a sample of Alumni Associations to name their key objectives for the year ahead. I guarantee you that engaging alumni, in one form or another, will likely appear at the top of the list.

It seems self-evident that Associations would and should be doing everything in their power to maximize alumni engagement, right?

But I am not remain completely convinced.

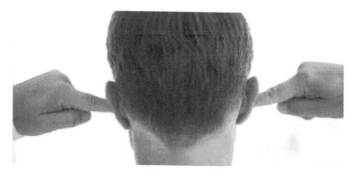

I think all Alumni Associations are of course interested in engaging alumni but some are sometimes held back because they are concerned about:

1. Complaints from their alumni

2. Negative comments being made about them or the alma mater

3. Or maybe the need to centrally control that engagement.

Yes, they want alumni engagement, but there may be some Associations who only want it if they can be guaranteed zero negativity.

This fear of taking risks when engaging alumni may mean that alumni engagement can never reach its full potential.

Let me provide some examples to illustrate my point.

Alumni Associations may be nervous about 'over-emailing' their alumni for fear of a minority of their alumni reacting negatively.

Or take a second example. Should alumni professionals allow an open discussion among alumni about what they would like to change?

Yes, there may be criticism and negativity, but it may also be the first important step in engaging alumni, and taking them on a journey to becoming active volunteers who care about the direction of your association, and are willing to get involved.

A successful alumni engagement strategy may require that we cease fearing our alumni.

I believe all engagement, even negative responses, will ultimately be positive.

We need to encourage and empower our alumni to take leadership roles and feel like owners.

We need to shift our thinking from risk-free alumni engagement to alumni empowerment.

The authentic voice of your Alumni Association is not the controlled alumni engagement that we may feel comfortable with.

The authentic voice is the combination of all those diverse voices and opinions.

The role of alumni professionals is to encourage all those voices to be heard, to empower those voices and converge them into one beautiful melody.

The role of alumni professionals is to be the conductor.

It's time we fully gave the microphone to our alumni. This is the bedrock of engaging alumni.

I would welcome your thoughts.

# Does The Alumni Relations Profession Have A Self-Esteem Issue?

Despite the somewhat provocative title to this blog, I think there is an issue in the alumni relations profession that is rarely spoken about; **low self-esteem.**

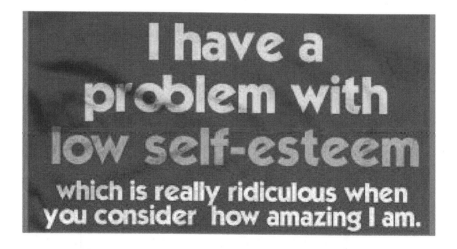

Interestingly, I mean low self-esteem not as individuals in a personal capacity, but rather as a profession.

In short, I believe there are some education institutions that doubt whether they have something of value to offer their alumni.

To illustrate my point, ask an average alumni relations professional the following question - what is the unique value proposition that you offer your alumni? A unique value proposition that your alumni cannot get from any other place, and something that they truly value? I think some would struggle to come up with a compelling answer.

Yet every education institution has the potential to offer a unique value proposition to their alumni; namely access to a life-long network. This life-long alumni network offers both a unique career community and a social alumni community. And almost as critically, it is also a network that is willing to help activate those opportunities.

My company Graduway's own research of more than 140,000 respondents shows that on average 70% of alumni are willing to help another alum in need. This is an extraordinarily high percentage and shows the value of alumni networking in general and alumni student mentoring in particular.

We live in a world where we are connected to millions of people via social networks, yet how willing is this vast network to help when I need it most? My guess is nowhere near that magical '70%' number.

Every education institution can provide a unique value proposition by offering access to a network that is willing to help and fill a huge void in the social and professional lives of their alumni.

The new networking principle is not who you know, but how willing your network is to help. Schools and colleges can be the facilitators and enablers of this new networking.

Let me leave you with my favorite 'self-esteem' quote from Yogi Bhajan:

"You are very powerful, provided you know how powerful you are."

I would welcome your thoughts.

# Is The Alumni Relations Profession Being Hijacked?

Every now and again one comes across something so profound that you must implore your colleagues to see and hear it for themselves.

The interview by Robert Curtis (VP Graduway) of Christine Fairchild, (Director of Alumni Relations at the University of Oxford) and Howard Wolf, (Vice President for Alumni Affairs at Stanford University) fits into that category.

The interview entitled, "The Alumni Relations Professional - Where Exactly Are We Headed?" was held at Oxford University at the 2015 Global Leaders Summit (GLS).

Christine and Howard bravely outline exactly where they think the profession is headed. Please watch the full footage on Graduway's YouTube channel: Global Leaders Summit 2015 Howard Wolf & Christine Fairchild.

Let me try and summarize the three key trends that were raised:

1. **Dealing With Disintermediation And Deepening The Value Proposition -** the growth of social networks like Facebook and LinkedIn continue to make the role of Alumni Relations no longer the central conduit that it once was. (It's also worth watching Andrew Gossen's keynote about disintermediation – see Graduway's YouTube channel: Global Leaders Summit 2014 - Andrew Gossen). In response to disintermediation, schools need to show their impact beyond 'bums on seats' at events, and think more about

their contribution towards the strategic goals of the institution i.e. recruiting top students, improving employment, and creating worthy ambassadors.

No longer can schools be seen as glorified party organizers.

**2. A Maniacal Focus On Return On Investment (ROI)** - Boards of Trustees sometimes see the University through the lens of a business. Should a University really be run like a business? Universities are not businesses, and alumni offices are not businesses. Certainly, they need to be run in a more business-like manner but they should not be run like a business. The implication of running an alumni association only as a business would be to identify alumni who are most involved and put disproportionate resources behind them. The flip side would be even more alarming - to write off those who will never be 'involved'. Why would you keep talking to customers that are never going to buy your product?

In short, if schools were only a business, Alumni Relations would only put resources into people who will provide an ROI.

But that is not the business that alumni offices are in. Boards run by successful business people don't seem to get?

Alumni Relations is about building a community. About the need to engage all alumni, irrespective of their desire, willingness or ability to give.

**3. Alumni Relations Being Subjugated to Development** - there has been a degradation in perceived value of Alumni Relations and that its only value is as a means to an end; and that end is financial giving. Part of this trend is driven by the fact that on average, University Presidents are only in their role for 7 years, and one of the few things that can bear fruit as a metric during their term is giving.

It feels like Alumni Relations and higher education generally are being hijacked.

This trend is particularly acute in US public institutions where Alumni Relations offices are becoming a division of the development office and subjugated to their goals. This will ultimately mean that we really are only reaching out to our alumni for one reason.

Christine and Howard boldly describe exactly where we are headed unless the profession can start to better communicate its value.

I would like to conclude with an Apple analogy that Howard provided which I think was particularly telling.

Apple spends billions of dollars each year, not in selling a product but selling the concept of being part of the Apple family. Often there is no clear ROI on this expenditure. Consumers once bought into the Apple brand, go on to participate and purchase various Apple products.

Imagine that Alumni Relations is the Corporate Brand Marketing arm of your organization. If Alumni Relations is no longer its own division, and simply reports into the development head, then your role becomes one of supporting the specific divisional product - and that product is giving.

Alumni are already distrustful of outreach from Universities - believing everything has a fundraising agenda even when this is not the case.

As a profession, we need to stand up for our constituents.

The relationship with alumni must be bi-directional. It must not be about just how alumni can help their alma mater. In fact, there is a long-term risk that the combination of these three trends is endangering and undermining the alumni loyalty to our institutions that took generations to build.

Alumni Relations needs to be advocating for the long-term game - the one of building a life-long loyal community.

Where do you think the profession is headed?

Do you agree with the thoughts expressed by Christine and Howard, or do you think they over-state the risk?

Do you think there are other critical trends facing the profession?

Finally, how do you think Alumni Relations professionals can better communicate their value?

I would welcome your thoughts.

# Get in touch!

I hope you found the articles in this book helpful.

I would be delighted to hear your thoughts and observations.

You can reach me at Daniel.Cohen@Graduway.com .

I look forward to hearing from you,


Daniel